SCHIRMER'S LIBRARY
OF MUSICAL CLASSICS

Vol. 1979

WOLFGANG AMADEUS MOZART

Variations

For Piano

ISBN 978-0-7935-2067-1

G. SCHIRMER, *Inc.*

DISTRIBUTED BY

HAL•LEONARD®
CORPORATION

7777 W. BLUEMOUND RD. P.O. BOX 13819 MILWAUKEE, WI 53213

Mozart's Variations for Piano offer a remarkably informative diary of his entire creative life. From K. 24 of the nine-year old prodigy to the K. 613 "Schikaneder" set composed only a few months prior to his death, these variations reveal the ideas and traits that have come to be known as Mozart's unique style. The variations are typically more virtuosic than the Sonatas, often recalling the bravura of the Concertos and the charm of some of his chamber works. Frequently, there are striking passages of innovation and daring. Variation VIII of K. 264 is an early example of the rich, almost free-form improvisatory style in which Mozart seemed to delight in the developmental sections of his sonatas, while Variation VII of K. 455 sounds as if it might have been a sketch for one of the late Sonatas of Beethoven. The Variations are ripe with virtuosic cadenzas and interpolated, cadenza-like extemporizations in *brillante* style. For example, in the cadenza of K. 264 there is even a *glissando* in parallel sixths. These variations for piano were often composed in groups of two or even three at a time, presumably for Mozart's own use as a virtuoso. They are then, perhaps, the quintessential expression of some of the infamous aspects of Mozart's character; the Variations are full of bravado, wit, and charm, but always controlled by the technical perfection of the master's hand.

Contents

8 VARIATIONS

on *Laat Ons Juichen* by C. E. Graaf
K.24

Wolfgang Amadeus Mozart
(1756-1791)

TEMA
Allegretto

VAR. I

7 VARIATIONS
on *Willem van Nassau*
K.25

VAR. III

VAR. IV

VAR. V
Adagio

VAR. VI
Tempo I

12 VARIATIONS
on a Minuet
from *Oboe Concerto No. 1* by J.C. Fischer
K.179

VAR. II

VAR. III

VAR. IV

VAR. V

VAR.VI

VAR.VII

VAR.VIII

VAR. IX

VAR. XII
Allegro

6 VARIATIONS

on *Mio caro Adone*

from *La Fiera di Venezia* by Salieri

K.180

VAR.III

VAR. VI
Allegretto

9 VARIATIONS

on *Lison dormait, Dans Un Bocage*

from *Julie* by Dezéde

K.264

VAR.IV

Tempo I

VAR. VI
Maggiore

VAR. IX
Allegro

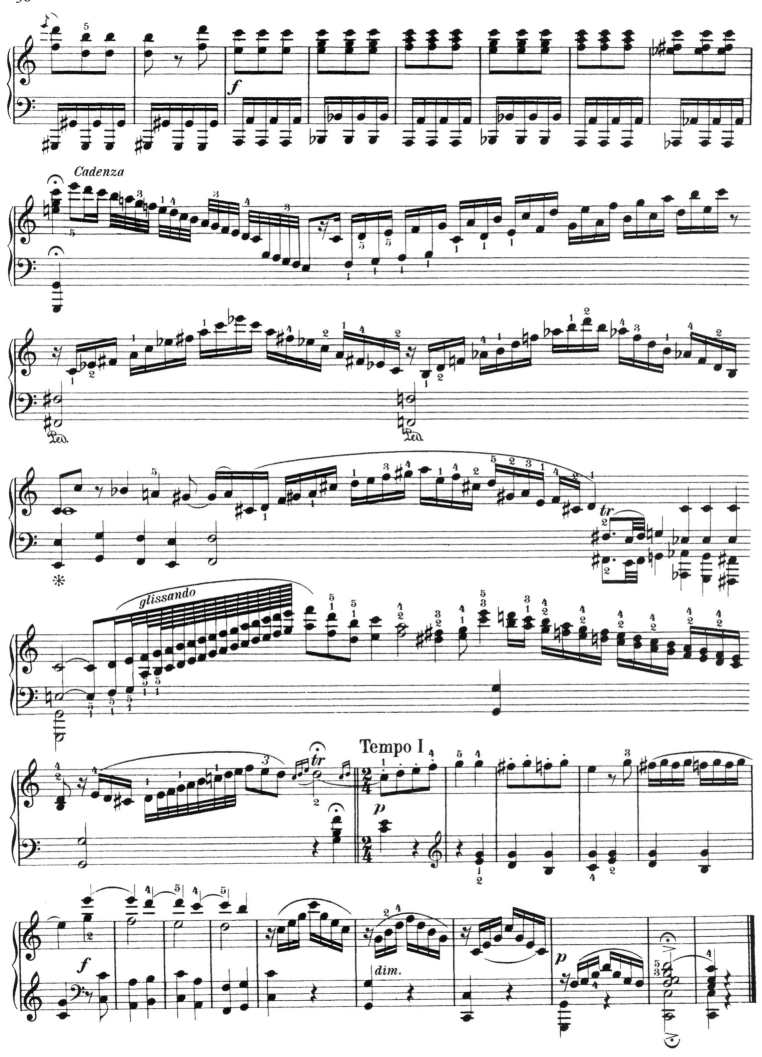

12 VARIATIONS

on *Ah, vous dirai-je, Maman*

K.265

VAR. XII
Allegro

8 VARIATIONS
on *Dieu d'amour*
from *Les Mariages Samnites* by Grétry
K.352

VAR. VIII
Allegro

12 VARIATIONS

on *La Belle Françoise*

K.353

VAR. XII
Presto

Tempo primo

12 VARIATIONS

on *Je suis Lindor* by Baudron
from Beaumarchais' *Le Barber de Séville*
K.354

VAR. II

legato

VAR. III

VAR. IV

VAR. V

VAR. VI

VAR. VII
Maestoso

VAR. VIII
Minore

VAR. IX
Maggiore

VAR. XI
Molto adagio

cantabile

VAR. XII
Tempo di Menuetto

Presto

Lento

6 VARIATIONS

on *Salve tu, Domine*

from *I Filosofi Immaginarii* by Paisello

K.398

VAR. II

Adagio

VAR. V
Maggiore
Tempo primo

10 VARIATIONS

on *Les Hommes Pieusement*
from *La Recontre Imprévue* by Gluck
K.455

VAR. VIII

VAR. IX
Adagio

VAR. X
Allegro

10 VARIATIONS
on *Come un agnello*
from *Fra I Due Litiganti* by Sarti
K.460

VAR.VII
Allegro

VAR. IX

espressivo

VAR. X
Allegro

12 VARIATIONS
on an original Allegretto
K.500

9 VARIATIONS

on a Minuet

from *Sonata for Violoncello*, Op.4 No.6 by Duport

K.573

VAR. III

VAR. IV

VAR.VI
Minore

VAR.VII
Maggiore

VAR. VIII
Adagio

VAR. IX
Allegro

8 VARIATIONS

on *Ein Weib ist das herrlichste Ding*
by Schack and/or Gerl from Schikaneder's *Der Dumme Gartner*
K.613

VAR. III

VAR. VII

Adagio

VAR. VIII
Allegro